Old GRANGEMOUTH

by

James Murphy

GRANGEMOUTH FROM THE AIR

A 65010 J.v.

First published in the United Kingdom, 2000,
by Stenlake Publishing, Ochiltree Sawmill, The Lade,
Ochiltree, Ayrshire, KA18 2NX
Telephone / Fax: 01290 423114

ISBN 1 84033 112 7

Some of the material in this book came from records held by Falkirk District Libraries and oral history collected from the former Monday Care Club for the frail elderly which was run by the Community Care Group of Grangemouth Council of Churches. Also consulted were back editions of the *Falkirk Herald* and *Grangemouth Advertiser* and Bob Porteous' books, *Grangemouth's Ancient Heritage* (1967) and *Grangemouth's Modern History* (1970).

ACKNOWLEDGEMENTS

The publishers wish to thank Chick and Carol Laing of Grangemouth for supplying most of the pictures in this book and also Robert Grieves for supplying the picture on page 25.

In 1877 the town's first fire station opened in Middle Street – the fire engine cost £155. Initially, its fortunes were rather chequered. In 1880 it could not attend a fire at Overton Farm as the harness for the horses had been lost and in 1887 disaster struck when all the brigade's horses perished in a fire at the burgh stables. The engine is pictured in North Basin Street, pumping water from the Sealock.

Previous page: Grangemouth, 1919. Between 1782 and 1972, 543 ships were built here. These included the world's first practical steamship, the *Charlotte Dundas*, which was the invention of William Symington. On completion of the first version of the ship, it was found that its engine (built at the Carron Ironworks) did not generate enough power and Symington had to build a second version which he successfully steamed up the Forth and Clyde Canal to Port Dundas in 1802. However, the Canal Company refused to take up their option to buy the ship as they thought the wash generated by it would damage the canal banks, so Symington sold it to Carron Ironworks to try and clear the debts created by its construction. It was used as a dredger before finally being left to rot. Ironically, by the time Symington died in poverty in 1831, the canal company had revised their opinion and were running cruises on the canal using a steam pleasure craft called the *Lord Dundas*. A memorial to Symington and his invention is in St Botolph's Church, London, and a model of his ship can be seen in Glasgow's Transport Museum.

INTRODUCTION

Grangemouth was officially born on 10 July, 1768, when Laurence Dundas cut the first sod to start the building of the Forth and Clyde Canal. But the history of the area stretches back to Roman times when the guards of Emperor Antonine's Mumrils Camp on the Antonine Wall built two caers (forward fortified defence posts) which became East and West Kerse. Thereafter, the strategic importance of the area between the River Avon and the River Carron was signified by the various battles fought there: in AD 574 King Aidan of Dalriada drove out the Saxons, Donal Breac of Dalriada was defeated by the Angles in AD 654, and in AD 711 the Picts and the Scots defeated the Northumbrians.

Around the middle of the twelfth century the monks of Arbroath Abbey panned for salt at Panstead and at East, Mid and West Saltcoats, sites all long lost under the docks and the B.P. works. Around this time King David I gave East Kerse to the monks of Newbattle for farming and also introduced Norman settlers to the land. One of them, John de Strivelyn, made his home at West Kerse. The family changed their name to Stirling and built Kerse Castle.

In 1347 Marjory Stirling inherited the estate and she married John de Mentieth, the grandson of the man who betrayed William Wallace. The Menteiths stayed until 1631, when King Charles I confiscated their lands for their refusal to conform to the Protestant religion, and Sir Thomas Hope, Lord Advocate of Scotland, bought the estate. He replaced the castle with Kerse Mansion and became famous in 1637 as one of the early defenders of the Covenanter's movement who instigated Jenny Geddes's riot in St Giles' Cathedral when the Episcopal bishop of Edinburgh tried to present the New Order of Service introduced by the King.

In 1752 Laurence Dundas bought the estate. Dundas had supplied the uniforms for the Duke of Cumberland's troops who fought at Culloden. He then became full quartermaster to Cumberland during the Seven Years War in Flanders and was made a Baronet of Great Britain for his services. As well as starting the canal, he was also a founding member of the Royal Bank of Scotland and initiated the building of Edinburgh's New Town.

Dundas also acquired the estates and titles of the Zetland family of Sutherland and when he died in 1782 he left all of his estates to his son, Thomas, who went on to build Grangemouth proper. Work started with Grange Lane and after North and South Charlotte streets were completed, he decided that all future houses would have gardens, hoping to create a garden city.

The town's position on the Firth of Forth made it ideal as a site for shipbuilding. In 1782 the first ship, *Jean and Janet*, was completed by J. Welsh and the following year ships were registered at the town for the first time. Associated industries sprung up in the form of a whale-boiling plant in North Basin Street, followed by a fish curing plant at the end of Middle Street. A ropeworks and sail maker were also established. In 1790 the canal opened and the import and export trade from Glasgow to the Continent really took off. The Carron Ironworks, established in 1759, also benefited from the canal.

Development continued throughout the nineteenth century with the opening of the gasworks, powered by the first of the five coal pits to be opened on the west side of the River Carron. A brickworks followed in 1861 and in the same year Union Place became the first street in the New Town, which would continue to expand with the increase of population. On 31 December, 1872, Grangemouth became a burgh with the power to elect its own councillors and the reigns of the Earls of Zetland came to an end.

At that time there was a population of 3,000, lubricated by twelve licensed premises in the Auld Toon alone! The docks expanded and the timber trade increased with a growing number of sawmills. The New Town also continued to grow in order to accommodate the increasing population and local services improved in tandem: four churches – West, Grange, Charing Cross and the Parish; three schools – Zetland, Dundas and Grange; a town hall; and the Victoria Public Library.

In 1867 the Caledonian Railway Company took over the canal and the docks and by the turn of the century trade had expanded so much that a new dock was built. This opened in 1906 with the launching of the R.M.S. *Scotland*. This period also saw the opening of the Y.M.C.A., Grandsable Cemetery, the Sacred Heart School, an infant school, the High School, and the moving of the Grange Church from the Auld Toon to Park Street.

The first chemical plant, the S.C.W.S. soapworks, arrived, followed by an oil and paraffin storage plant at the docks for the Anglo-American Oil Company. Ross Creosote Company and the B.P. Oil Company were also established at the docks (the latter was a German registered company and not British Petroleum). Scottish Dyes arrived in 1919 and the Scottish Oils Refinery started operation in 1924. This continual increase in industry led directly to the rise in population: in 1923, when the first council house was built in South Marshall Street, the population was 10,031 and by 1938 there were 1,000 council houses and a population of 13,532.

After the Second World War, industrial growth continued. In the 1950s, I.C.I. – which had taken over the Dyes – doubled its capacity. B.P. (British Petroleum) started chemical production at this time and Glasgow overspill increased the population so much that Grangemouth was getting a name as a boom town.

Since regionalisation in 1975 and the recent local authority reorganisation (Grangemouth is now under the supervision of Falkirk District), however, many local people feel that the town is much worse off than in former years. Despite the high contribution the town and its industry makes towards the region's taxation, the town seems to see little in return. Many people now shop out of town and many workers commute in from other areas rather than live locally.

However, as the success of Grangemouth Heritage Trust and its collection of local artefacts and memorabilia shows, there is great and growing interest in Grangemouth's proud past and it is hoped that this book will serve as a reminder of it.

On 28 July, 1790, the Forth and Clyde Canal was officially opened by the pouring of a hogshead of water from the Firth of Forth into the River Clyde. In 1797 Kerse Road was opened, running from Polmont to Glensburgh, and the building on the left was the road's toll house and home of the keeper of Dalgrain Bridge. A wooden bascule probably built around the time the canal opened, it was destroyed in 1933 when a steam truck carrying a load of cobbles crashed through it and into the water. It was replaced by a swing bridge. At midnight on 31 December, 1962, the canal was closed to commercial use. It was drained in 1966 and a road was built in its place at this site. The area in the picture was almost in the back garden of the Dundas Estate. It became the site of the Dyes' recreation club in 1932, much to the disgust of an old worthy, Maggie Cannon, who used to go berry picking there to raise money to buy her family Christmas presents.

In this view from 1947, the ship on the stocks is the S.S. *Thisbe* which was being built for the French government. The white building left of centre, at the end of the row, was the dockyard office where long queues of workers formed every Friday to collect their pay. All the houses further down the row have been demolished and replaced by the Jarvie Plant depot. Halfway down Canal Street was the entrance to Burnett Street, the smallest street in the town which housed its first school. Opened by Lord Dundas in 1789, there was also a house for the schoolmaster who was paid £5 a year. This salary was supplemented by fees of between four and six shillings from each of his pupils. A new school, the Zetland, was built around 1808 on the corner of Green Street and Middle Street and in 1913 this was replaced by another with the same name in Middle Street. This closed just a few years ago.

CANAL STREET AND DOCKYARD, GRANGEMOUTH.

B.2428

Canal Street, Grangemouth.

The opposite end of Canal Street a few decades earlier. On the right are the premises of Young's the cobblers who later moved to Dundas Street. The Hay family lived next door in the second house from the right. Wee Nellie Hay, now aged 96, was nicknamed by her school chums 'Hay's-Guid-For-Horses' as she used to feed her piece from her ground floor window to the horses who were released here after pulling canal barges from Lock 16 in Camelon. On the left the timber rafts are waiting to go into the 'Splash', the entrance into the timber basins.

The Sealock at the end of Canal Street marked the start of the canal. The building in the centre of the picture housed Willie Boyle's Ship Inn. At one time the tallest building in Grangemouth, it was known as the 'Highlands' because the first tenants were not used to climbing so many stairs. The Zetland Arms Hotel on the right was built in 1858. This picture dates from 1911 and the horse and cart was the 'soor-milk cairt' from Bothkennar. A later milkman in the 1920s and '30s was Davey Dobbie – his name was actually Jimmy but everybody just called him by the name of the original milkman. When he finished his round here he always gave his horse a bowl of beer while having his own refreshment. In the afternoon he delivered fruit and vegetables and finished his round at the top end of Dalgrain Road. The horse was called Danny and when Davey started to sing 'Danny Boy', it was trained to take off at a fine trot back to its stable.

The Carron Dock was officially opened by Alexander Thomson in 1843. A timber merchant and ship owner, Thomson established his firm next door to the granary on North Charlotte Street and his ship, the *Hampton*, sailing from Quebec with a cargo of grain, was the first to arrive at the dock. The exit from the dock into the River Carron could be a little difficult at times, as was proved in 1898 when the S.S. *St Blicher* – recently built at the dockyard and going down stream on her trials – collided with the Norwegian steamer *Frigg*. As a result the *Frigg* rammed and sank a fishing smack from the Isle of Man. The *Frigg* itself was only slighty damaged while the *St Blicher* had to have new plates installed before finishing her trials. Four days after this incident the *Dunmore*, outward bound at the same point, collided with the *Thomas Haynes* and plans were drawn up shortly after for a new dock that would open directly into the Forth. This was completed in 1906.

Lighthouse and S.S. Orient, Grangemouth.

Just after the opening of the Carron Dock, a lighthouse was built opposite its entrance to ease navigation. It remained in use until the new dock was opened and finally fell into ruin during the Second World War. Over the years some great fishing was done around here and in December 1849 it was reported that some of Mr Adamson's men from the Dockyard caught a conger eel measuring five feet in length and 22 inches around its thickest part.

The Caledonian Railway Company installed electricity at the docks in 1884 and Grangemouth was the first port in Scotland to have electric cranes. The power station is on the right. The docks were the scene of controversy in 1897 when protesters tried to stop the export of live horses to Germany for sausage making. Banner-carrying women from Glasgow came through by train to form a human barrier to stop the horses entering the docks. These were retired tram horses from Glasgow and the trade lasted until 1905.

Timber has been one of the biggest imports to Grangemouth, especially from the Baltic, America and Canada. Timber companies based in Grangemouth included McPherson & McLaren, Dow's (later Muirhead's, then Stanton's, and now Finn Forest), and Brownlee's which later became International Timber. Pit-props were also imported by Abercrombie, Brisbane & Brown and by Gibb & Austine.

Muirhead's pipe band on parade in Dalgrain Park. Established in 1928, it was initially known as Burn's Boys Band. Their heyday was in the 1960s when they won the world championship nine times, including five in a row. In those years the band also welcomed Prince Philip and the Queen to the town and they played at Balmoral as her personal guests. They performed regularly at Celtic music festivals in Brittany and even appeared in the James Bond movie, *Casino Royale*. Although they were disbanded in 1978, their playing can still be enjoyed on the records they made in their glory days.

THE DOCKS, GRANGEMOUTH.

A.4544.

When the First World War broke out, the Admiralty took over Grangemouth docks and closed them to commercial use. It was used as a base for 'Q' Ships, which were used to hunt U Boats. One of them, H.M.S. *Heather*, a corvette disguised as a coaster and which had been built in the dockyard, sank five U Boats during the winter of 1917–18. The ship's captain, Lt. Commander Auten, won the Victoria Cross. This is a view of the new dock from 1936. On the left is the tugs' jetty. The bridge in the centre, probably built in 1906 as part of the new dock, was the first electrically operated bridge in Scotland and became even more famous when the titles of the film *A Bridge Too Far* were superimposed over a view of it. The bridge still stands but is no longer in use.

13

The S.S. *Carron* sailed between Grangemouth and Scotland Yard in London three times a week. Apart from these long distance steamers, pleasure steamers also used to sail from the town on trips up and down the Firth of Forth. In 1922, one such boat, the *Forth*, carrying a Salvation Army Sunday school outing, lost power and lay helpless for three hours until a tug came out to tow it back to the docks where hundreds of people gathered to greet it. Apparently, while stranded the passengers had been entertained by the Salvation Army band and, in *Titanic* style, they all joined in with 'Nearer my God to thee'.

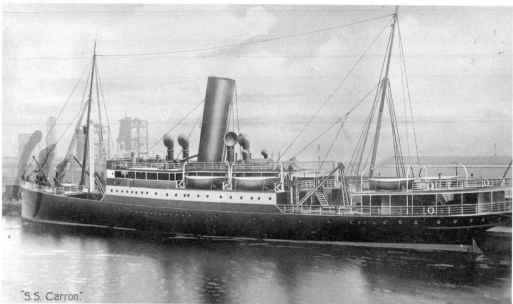

"S.S. Carron."

The Rankine Line steamer S.S. *Rotterdam*, built by Gourlay Brothers of Dundee in 1896. The Rankine Line ran two steamers a week from Grangemouth to Rotterdam. Cabin fares were £2 single and £3, ten shillings return. The ship had 44 first class cabins and room for 67 steerage passengers and could carry 1,000 tons of cargo. In 1924 she was sold to the Limerick Steamship Company and renamed *Clounanna*. She covered this company's Ireland to France route until 1929 when she was scrapped in Alloa.

14

In the 1920s and '30s the horse trough on Grange Street was the rendezvous for the Salvation Army Band who played there every Saturday night. On many occasions 'Cobbler' Ellis would stagger out of the Railway Bar opposite, throw his loose change on to the big drum which the band used as a collection plate and demand 'Bringing in the Sheaves'. He would then lead the singing and, often, Constables Valentine and Burnett would have to lead him off round the corner to the cells. He would sober up overnight and pay for his 'board' by cobbling the policemen's boots. He was nicknamed 'Pawn-the-hammer' as he pawned his tools to buy his drink.

Grange Street was well off for pubs and besides the Railway Bar, there was also the Baltic, Burn's Tavern and the Royal Hotel. In the early years of the twentieth century shops on the street included three drapers – Ballantyne's, Hendrie's and Walker's; three grocers – Wm. Low's, Christie's and Findlay's; four newsagents – Allan's, Cameron's, Hannah's and Tailor Walker & Co.; two hairdressers – Crookson's and Whittle's; and finally there was also Grassom's furniture store.

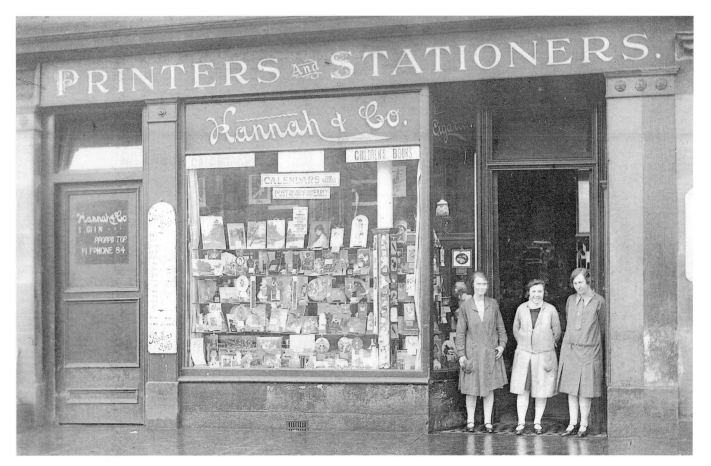

Hannah's opened in Grange Street around 1904. Later they moved to Charing Cross and then to Dundas Street where they are still in business. I used to buy cigarettes from the Charing Cross shop and on one occasion I was buying my usual – twenty Senior Service – when a travelling salesman who was there asked if I bought the brand regularly. I said yes and he answered, "Well, the next time ask for them by name and let the other customers hear you," and with that he handed me a box of a hundred cigarettes. The next night I was in the Shakespeare Bar in Lothian Road, Edinburgh. I asked for a Drambuie and a gentleman next to me told the barman to give me a Glavya and paid for it. He asked me what I thought of it. "A bit sweet, but I might get used to it" I replied, so he bought me another and then presented me with a half bottle of Glavya out of his bag. "Now don't forget," he said, "the next time you are in here order a Glavya and let the punters hear you." You don't get salesmen like that anymore and when I go into Hannah's, I remember those occasions.

Bridge Street, Grangemouth.

Along with Grange Street, South Bridge Street was the hub of the Auld Toon's shopping district with bakers, hairdressers, cafes, the Queen's Hotel, the Co-op's 'Big Store', and the chemist run firstly by Mr Baxter and then by Mr Wood. A very old bottle of medicine from Wood's is on show in the Heritage Centre.

Bread deliveries on South Bridge Street, *c.*1911. During the 1950s, when mopeds first came on the market, a lodger in Devlin's 'Model' used to park it among the timber in the yard on the right. However, some daring youngsters used to borrow it and ride it down Grange Lane, along South Charlotte Street to South Basin Street and back. One night, however, they disturbed the timber and were attacked by a family of rats that had nested there. After that, they never ventured back!

Bridge Street, Grangemouth.

The Town Hall and the 'Toon Knock' (clock), is on the left of this view of Bridge Street. This was replaced by a new hall at Charing Cross in 1885 and in 1900 the old hall became the home of the *Grangemouth Advertiser* until it moved to new premises in Kerse Road in 1912 (the *Falkirk Herald* later took over the paper). The building then became the 'Buroo'. The bascule bridge here gave access from the docks to the timber basins and was often very busy.

On the right is the Junction Dock from where timber rafts would be transferred to the basin. The bridge was opened by an operator turning a wheel to raise it. Tragedy struck in 1931 when, while pulling a cart, the railway company's delivery horse galloped across the bridge before it was fully closed, causing the wheel to swing round at a terrible speed, battering the operator and throwing him into the dock. The operator, Adam Balloch, was killed.

The new bridge, built in 1938. When the canal and the timber basins were drained in 1966, Canal Street, the Basin Streets, and North and South Charlotte Streets were all demolished. Nothing was left of the Auld Toon except for the Zetland School, the police station and the Queen's Hotel. The school has since closed and the old police station was demolished only this year. A pressure group is trying to save the clock tower and it is probably only a matter of time before the hotel block goes. Dock warehouses now cover most of this area. Countless tales could be told about the Queen's and its punters, such as Sanny Inglis, the guard on a passenger train. Grangemouth pubs closed half an hour after the Falkirk ones and the last train from Falkirk brought in a fair number of drinkers. Sanny always made sure that the train was never late as he liked to join them in the hotel for last orders.

Station Road, Grangemouth

Station Brae was built in 1911 and on the left of the picture, above Rae's, were the premises of one of the town's best known shops, Hansen's Outfitters who were dealers in maritime clothing. During the 1920s the shop was raided by some German sailors from a ship in the docks – they were caught and ended up in court. Two weeks later Hansen himself was in court for illegally selling alcohol over his counter!

Charing Cross, Grangemouth.

One of the earliest motor bus services available to Grangemouth folk was the service between the town and Bo'ness run by Mrs Templeton, who ran the Queen's Hotel Garage. It left Grangemouth twice daily at 8.30 a.m. and 3.30 p.m. In 1919 services between Grangemouth and Falkirk were started by the Scottish General Transport Company of Larbert, an associate of the Falkirk and District Tramway Company. The bus pictured, no. 72, was one of the company's red liveried Tilling Stevens buses and was put into service brand new in 1924. In the background left is the Commercial Bank which was built in 1910. On its commission the *Advertiser* reported the plans of the new building: "The building is of the Roman order of architecture, finished on the top with pediments and ornamental balustrading. The front has a projecting portico surmounted by a tower with a copper covered dome roof in which there is a clock. . . . The finishings inside are of polished mahogany and will be heated by radiators." The bank closed in the 1950s and the building is now owned by an evangelical brethren group.

This is the same bus as on the previous page. In the 1920s one of the S.G.T's conductresses (not pictured!) appeared in court for having 44 passengers in her bus when the limit was 36. The judge said he had been too lenient in the past and in the future he would fine the passengers as well! Around the same time a bus driver was fined fifteen shillings for speeding at 18 m.p.h. and a further £3 for doing 25 m.p.h. on another occasion.

CHARING CROSS AND BO'NESS ROAD, GRANGEMOUTH

In 1887 Mrs Andrew Carnegie was invited to launch a ship at the docks and in thanks Andrew Carnegie gave a donation of £900 to the building of the Victoria Public Library (in the centre of the picture) which opened two years later. In 1905 Carnegie bought his first car, a Winton limousine, and his choice was influenced by its Scottish connection – Alexander Winton, a pioneer in the motor industry, was born in Grangemouth in 1860! Beyond the library is the Glenavon Hotel which opened in the early 1800s; it made way for the Municipal Buildings which were built in 1939. At the rear of the hotel were stables for stagecoach horses. In the 1830s the Canal Company introduced streamlined barges known as 'Swifts' which were pulled by teams of horses that were changed regularly to give fast passage between Glasgow and Lock 16. From there stagecoaches would convey the passengers to the steamships at Grangemouth going to Newhaven for Edinburgh. Henry Bell's *Comet*, another early steamship, was one of the boats that provided this service.

26

Dr Spenser in his famous car. The La Scala in the background right is a reminder that if he was needed on a Thursday evening he could always be found there in the front row of the balcony with 'Pin' Henderson, the tailor. The cinema was built in 1911 and was originally called the Electric. It stopped showing films in the 1960s but the building lives on as a well-patronised bingo hall. The manager of the La Scala, Mr Faulkner, had earlier run the 'Auld Gaff', the original parish church (built in 1866) which became a variety theatre and cinema when the congregation split (this led to the establishment of the Kerse Church and the building of a new parish church in 1911). Ebbie Clason was the caretaker of the Gaff and the front room of his house in Dundas Street was kept exclusively for the stars who were to appear there. Both Harry Houdini and Harry Lauder performed at the theatre and, before returning to America, Houdini left behind a hamper of his tricks which was inherited by Jimmy Gow who became a well-known magician in the town.

Charing Cross, La Scala Picture House and Town Hall, Grangemouth

To the right of the La Scala is the new town hall which was built in 1885. The building has been used for a variety of functions. In 1897, five hundred people dined there to celebrate the official opening of the S.C.W.S. soapworks and it was the venue for the welcome home parties for servicemen returning from the First World War. During the Second World War it housed R.A.F. personnel who were also often entertained there by the likes of Ivor Novello and Alistair Sim. The hall also saw the debut of Max Bygraves who was one of the airmen billeted in it. After the war, the Dundee Rep. appeared regularly at the hall (amongst the players was the young Virginia McKenna) and Grangemouth's Dramatic Club was also based at it – they won the National Drama Festival in 1960. During the Burgh centenary celebrations in 1972, international groups appeared at the hall, including variety shows, ballet performances and symphony concerts. Local events continue to be staged there, including concerts given by the Choral Society.

Lumley Street, Grangemouth.

Named after the family of one of Laurence Dundas' daughters-in-law, Lumley Street was the main road and shopping centre of the New Town. The restaurant on the left was called the Imperial and its hall at the rear now houses the Heritage Centre. In 1969 the redevelopment of the town centre began and this part of the street is now pedestrianised and called La Porte Precinct after Grangemouth's American twin town (a 'People to People' charter between the towns was signed in 1970).

The detached building in this view of York Place on Lumley Street was the premises of Hood's the photographers. It was later raised on to rollers and horses towed it into a new location on Talbot Street (the building was eventually removed during the redevelopment). On the left is Thomas Stevens, Outfitters – a great clothing store. One of his sons became well-known as an artist in stained glass and his work adorns the town's St Mary's Episcopal Church and the Kirk of the Holy Rood in the Bowhouse area.

Lumley Street, *c.1900*. On the right are the gates of Janeville, Dr Spenser's surgery. There is a story that in 1913 a young apprentice from Tennant's bakery cut his wrist badly and was rushed to the surgery for immediate treatment. Apparently, the doctor cleaned the wound and then stitched it with a horse hair he drew out from his sofa! During the First World War the house became H.M.S. *Rameses*, the H.Q. of the navy on the east coast of Scotland. After the war it became Dr Dyer's surgery, a dentist's surgery and the premises of two hairdresser's in succession. At the top of the street is Brownlee's timbermill at the docks. It moved to the site at Charing Cross later taken by the La Scala, and finally in 1904 to the site on Earls Road where the company still trades under the name of International Timber.

Lumley Street, Grangemouth.

The same view of Lumley Street a couple of decades later. On the left is Samson's the barbers, Willie Low's, Dollar's Chemist, Birrell's sweetie shop and Steven's Outfitters. On the right is Aitken's Ironmongers, the entrance to Talbot Street and then the Co-op's 'Big Store'. The Co-op grocery was on this street while around the corner was the entrance to their chemist. Upstairs was the hall where customers queued for their dividend.

The bowling green on Talbot Street was opened in 1883, replacing one that had been in use in the Auld Toon beside the canal and timber basin since 1820. In the background are Inch Cottage and Dundas Kirk. In times gone by the River Carron flowed around here, forming an island known as Inch Island. The bowling green is still much used today, but the curling pond run by the club, which was out of picture on the right, has long gone.

The Co-op on Kerse Road comprised of a bakery, grocery, the shoe shop and the mantle and drapery department – all so much a part of the life of the town from the 1920s through to the '60s, but alas, all now gone.

Ned Hotchkiss' chip-cairt, which before the Second World War sat just beyond the Co-op drapers in Kerse Road (the cart had a fireplace for cooking). For years it was a popular rendezvous for townsfolk. Across the road was the Boilermaker's Hall which was these workers' recreation hall, famous for dances and wedding receptions, as well as the meeting place for their union. Next to it was the printing works of the *Advertiser* and a close where bookies' runners would collect slips for illegal bets. The runners were often arrested and their takings forfeited. The *Advertiser* reported that in court one who was caught pleaded guilty and was given the choice of a £10 fine or sixty days in prison. He had been bailed for £10 so he gave up his bail money.

The Y.M.C.A. building on Abbots Road was opened in 1900. During the First World War this was the billet for the O.R.s (non-commissioned sailors) of the naval headquarters and in 1923 it was the venue of local man W. Falconer's world-record for weightlifting – a one hand clean and jerk lift of 114 lbs. At the Y.M.C.A. that same year there was also the first local demonstration of a crystal-set wireless and earphones. In 1992 it became the venue for the local Council of Churches Bosnia Appeal during which teams of volunteers from nine local churches packed 2,016 boxes of clothing, food, and medicines. The goods were delivered to Bosnia with the help of local hauliers, John Mitchell and Duncan Adams, and the Flanders Scottish Alliance. The churches also raised £1,200 to cover the fuel bills for the deliveries to Sarajevo. The Y.M.C.A. was demolished in 1995, but its doors (engraved with the name H.M.S. *Rameses*, put there when it was a billet) and its sports awards boards and trophies are now on show in the Heritage Centre.

The Grange School on the right was officially opened in 1894 by the local M.P., Mr McKillop. In 1906, by then no longer an M.P., he was involved in a public scandal when he appeared in court to testify at the trial of an employee of one of his companies who had somehow set up his own bank and misappropriated £4,000. A man of honour, McKillop settled the debt in private. In 1901 the school became the Grange Higher Grade School, an early type of high school, and when the High School itself opened in 1909 it became a girls' school. The Grange Church, behind the school, was originally based in the Auld Toon and moved to this location in Park Street in 1903. The congregation later joined with that of the Old Parish round the corner which became the present Zetland Parish Church. The Grange Church was later turned into flats. The school was demolished in 1998 and flats now occupy the site.

High School, Grangemouth.

An early brochure for the High School provides this information on the provisions of its curriculum: "A: supplementary classes for those who pass the 'Qualifying Examination', and intend to leave after reaching the legal age for leaving; B: for pupils, having passed the 'Qualifying Examination' and intend to stay for three years of secondary education, subjects per week will be: Religious Instruction – ½ hour; Arithmetic and Maths – 6¾ hours; English, including Geography and History – 7½ hours; Science – 3 hours; French 6¼ hours; Drawing/Manual Instruction – 3½ hours; Drill – 1½ hours; Singing – 1 hour." In the 1930s, eight singing pupils took part in a Royal Command Performance in the Royal Albert Hall in the presence of the King and Queen. One of the Art masters was Mr Davie, mysteriously nicknamed 'Nunkie', and one of his pupils, Jack Leyden, moved to South Africa and became a world famous cartoonist. His early cartoons for the *Natal Daily News* were always signed 'Nunkie 2'.

Zetland Park was gifted to the town by the Earl of Zetland in 1882 and it continues to be a great asset. The fountain has been moved about a hundred yards from its position here and the war memorial, erected in 1923, now stands in the central area of the picture. The roads on either side of the park – Abbots Road and Abbotsgrange Road – are a reminder of the land's use as Abbots Kerse.

THE CHILDREN'S POND, GRANGEMOUTH, PUBLIC PARK   A.4547.

The pond has been a great source of pleasure since it opened in 1931, being used for paddling, model yacht sailing and even skating in winter. On the left in the middle of the trees stood the grange (a church's granary) built by the monks of Holy Rood in Edinburgh. The burn there became the Grangeburn and when the canal was planned it was decided that it would run from Bowling to a sealock at Grangeburnmouth and that is how the town got its name.

The football team of the 1st Grangemouth Boys Brigade, season 1930/31. From this team to the Grange Rovers and then to Celtic and Blackpool, Willie Buchan (front row, second left) was one of the great names of Scottish football. He played 150 times for Celtic, scoring 61 goals including one that gave them a 1–0 victory over Aberdeen in the 1937 cup final. 143,433 spectators set up a record for attendance at that match but within a week the triumph was lost against Motherwell. Both the goalkeeper and the right back had gone off injured and Celtic were 4–0 down when Willie took over in goal. But his efforts couldn't save them and they lost 8–0. Blackpool paid a transfer fee of £10,000 for him, the highest ever paid at that time, and there he played alongside Stanley Matthews. During the war, while in the R.A.F., he guested for Manchester United and scored a hat trick against Blackpool. He worked for I.C.I. after retiring from the game and he later became the County Veteran Bowling Champion. Now in his mid-eighties, Willie still cycles nearly every day to his favourite haunts, the local library and the bookie's.

The town's biggest annual event is Children's Day. The first was in 1906 when 2,000 local children walked in procession to what is now the Dyes recreation grounds to run races and have a picnic. In 1907 and 1908 they paraded around the whole town to the park and in 1909 the first Queen, Nancy Baxter, was crowned. Except during the wars, there has been a parade and a crowning every year since.

Born in Grangemouth in 1922, George – 'Geordie' – Young played in the Zetland Park as a schoolboy and went on to win great fame with Rangers and Scotland. He signed for Rangers in 1941 and his debut for Scotland was a wartime international in 1943. He captained his country for the first time in 1948 and in 1953 he completed a run of 34 consecutive caps. He retired in 1957. Nicknamed 'Corky', he carried a champagne cork from a Rangers' cup final celebration wherever he went. He died in 1997. Here he is as a schoolboy with his early sporting caps; his first cap for Scotland is on view at the Heritage Centre.

1909 – Semi-Jubilee – 1933

GRANGEMOUTH
CHILDREN'S DAY
SATURDAY
17th JUNE, 1933

QUEEN MABEL MALCOLMSON.

Looking down towards the park, this part of the Grange burn (which was tidal) was a swimming place of long standing. During the building of the new dock an artificial lake was built on the right of this picture and the burn water was pumped into the lake, but after the opening of the dock the burn was restored and water still flows along it today. Kingseat Avenue bridge now crosses the burn here.

THE SWIMMING POOL, GRANGEMOUTH.   A.4536.

The swimming pool, pictured here in 1936, was built in the 1920s and initially old railway coaches were used as changing rooms. Proper cubicles and surrounding walls were erected in 1932. The pool was open to the elements but a great number of locals were taught to swim there. Many may still remember the pool managers old Finlayson and Christine Orr. Christine died a few years ago and in her will left her trophies and medals to the Heritage Centre. The present children's playground now covers this site and a new pool complex has been built on the right of the Grange burn.

Bo'ness Road was the main road to the east and its Victorian mansions housed company executives, dentists, doctors and ministers. Behind the trees at the far end of the road on the right is Lea Park, whose owners have included the Millars of the Dockyard Company and Hans Fischer, the ship owner who also built Mahratta Villa which is just out of picture on the immediate left. Other houses on the road include Avon Dhu (just out of picture on the right), built by Mr McLaren of McPherson & McLaren the timber merchants, which has been converted into flats, and next door to it, Avon Hall which was home of the Fairley family who were also in the timber business. B.P. now own the house and use it as a conference centre.

THE CENTRAL SCOTLAND AIRPORT, GRANGEMOUTH.

In 1931 an 'air circus' was held on the lands of Reddoch farm and it was suggested that the area would be an excellent place for an airport. Reddoch, Claret, Wholeflats Abbotsgrange and Bowhouse farms all became the site of the airport which began construction in February 1939 and was completed by 28 April the same year. The official opening of the Central Scotland Airport took place the following July. Lord Trenchard, head of the R.A.F., performed the ceremony and a Dakota airliner belonging to K.L.M. was the first plane to land. One of the earliest services was a shuttle flight to London. Passengers from Glasgow and Edinburgh were collected by bus at Polmont Station and conveyed to the airport for the flight on a De Havilland Rapide aircraft. The fare was £9, 10 shillings return.

46

THE CENTRAL SCOTLAND AIRPORT, GRANGEMOUTH.

A.8748.

The airport's days of commercial use were short-lived as war broke out in September, 1939. The R.A.F. took it over for use as a flying school for pilots from nearly all over the world. Tiger Moths were the main training planes. Fifty-eight airmen who lost their lives mostly in training accidents are buried in a garden of remembrance at the local cemetery at Grandsable. Four air aces, including a Canadian, two New Zealanders, and the famous Neville Duke, all tell of their training days at the school in their biographies. In 1947, the aerodrome became a flying school for the R.A.F. Volunteer Reserve. By 1950 flights were very few and far between; go-cart racing took place on the runaways and a dog track was proposed for the site. However, this was rejected in favour of the land becoming the site of overspill housing for incomers from Glasgow. Work on the housing began in 1954 and the last flight took off the following year. Hangars 1 and 2 are still in use today as a transport warehouse and Falkirk District's museum workshops respectively.

B.H.C. WORKS, GRANGEMOUTH

D 7381

In 1948 Wimpey began the construction of the British Hydrocarbon Chemicals plant. A pit bing in Bo'ness and the shale bings of Uphall provided the bottoming for the foundations. The plant went into operation in 1951, the first of the petrochemical plants that dominate the east side of the town.